The Beautiful Changes

THE
BEAUTIFUL
CHANGES

And Other Poems
By Richard Wilbur

Reynal & Hitchcock, New York

ACKNOWLEDGMENT

Certain of these poems have appeared in *Accent, Foreground, Harvard Advocate, Junior Bazaar, New Directions No. 10,* and *Poetry Quarterly* (London).

Printed in the U.S.A. by the Cornwall Press, Inc. ◄►I

Contents

For Charlee

CIGALES

You know those windless summer evenings, swollen to stasis
by too-substantial melodies, rich as a
running-down record, ground round
to full quiet. Even the leaves
have thick tongues.

And if the first crickets quicken then,
other inhabitants, at window or door
or rising from table, feel in the lungs
a slim false-freshness, by this
trick of the ear.

Chanters of miracles took for a simple sign
the Latin cigale, because of his long waiting
and sweet change in daylight, and his singing
all his life, pinched on the ash leaf,
heedless of ants.

Others made morals; all were puzzled and joyed
by this gratuitous song. Such a plain thing
morals could not surround, nor listening:
not "chirr" nor "cri-cri." There is no straight
way of approaching it.

This thin uncomprehended song it is
springs healing questions into binding air.
Fabre, by firing all the municipal cannon
under a piping tree, found out
cigales cannot hear.

WATER WALKER

There was an infidel who
Walked past all churches crying,
Yet wouldn't have changed his tears,
Not for the smoothest-worn pew;
You've seen
Caddis flies walking on spring-surface, water walkers who breathe
Air and know water, with weakly wings
Drying to pelt and sheen;

There is something they mean

By breaking from water and flying
Lightly some hours in air,
Then to the water-top dropping,
Floating their heirs and dying:
It's like
Paulsaul the Jew born in Tarshish, who when at bay on the steps
With Hebrew intrigued those Jewsotted Jews
Crowding to stone and strike;

Always alike and unlike,

Walking the point where air
Mists into water, and knowing
Both, with his breath, to be real,
Roman he went everywhere:
I've been
Down in Virginia at night, I remember an evening door
A table lamp lit; light stretched on the lawn,
Seeming to ask me in;

I thought if I should begin

To enter entirely that door,
Saying, "I am a son of this house,

My birth and my love are here,"
I might never come forth any more:
Air mists
Into water, past odors of halls and the fade of familial voices,
Stair creaks, piano tones falling on rugs,
Wallpaper palimpsests:

Armored the larva rests

Dreaming the streambottom tides,
Writhing at times to respire, and
Sealing to him flat stones,
He closely abides, abides:
One night
I sat till dawn on a porch, rocked in a cane-bottom chair,
In Geneseo, in Illinois,
Rocking from light to light;

Silent and out of sight

I saw the houses sleep
And the autos beside them sleeping,
The neat plots, the like trustful houses,
Minute, armoreal, deep;
Wind went
Tamely and samely as puppies, tousling the Japanese maples,
Lawnsprays and tricycles waited for sun,
Shyly things said what they meant:

An old man stitching a tent

Could have been Saul in Tharsos,
Loved and revered; instead
He carried Jew visions to Greeks
For adoration or curses;
For he
Troubled them; whether they called him "babbler" or hailed him
"Mercurios"

(Scarcely restrained from killing him oxen),
His wasn't light company:

Still pearled with water, to be

Ravished by air makes him grow
Stranger to both, and discover
Heaven and hell in the poise
Betwixt "inhabit" and "know";
I hold
Here in my head Maine's bit speech, lithe laughter of Mobile blacks,
Opinions of salesmen, ripe tones of priests,
Plaints of the bought and sold:

Can I rest and observe unfold

The imminent singletax state,
The Negro rebellion, the rise
Of the nudist cult, the return
Of the Habsburgs, watch and wait
And praise
The spirit and not the cause, and neatly precipitate
What is not doctrine, what is not bound
To enclosured ground; what stays?

Lives that the caddis fly lays

Twixt air and water, must lie
Long under water—how Saul
Cursed once the market babblers,
Righteous could watch them die!
Who learns
How hid the trick is of justice, cannot go home, nor can leave,
But the dilemma, cherished, tyrannical,
While he despairs and burns

Da capo da capo returns.

TYWATER

Death of Sir Nihil, book the *nth*,
Upon the charred and clotted sward,
Lacking the lily of our Lord,
Alases of the hyacinth.

Could flicker from behind his ear
A whistling silver throwing knife
And with a holler punch the life
Out of a swallow in the air.

Behind the lariat's butterfly
Shuttled his white and gritted grin,
And cuts of sky would roll within
The noose-hole, when he spun it high.

The violent, neat and practiced skill
Was all he loved and all he learned;
When he was hit, his body turned
To clumsy dirt before it fell.

And what to say of him, God knows.
Such violence. And such repose.

MINED COUNTRY

They have gone into the gray hills quilled with birches,
Drag now their cannon up the chill mountains;
But it's going to be long before
Their war's gone for good.

I tell you it hits at childhood more than churches
Full up with sky or buried town fountains,
Rooms laid open or anything
Cut stone or cut wood,

Seeing the boys come swinging slow over the grass
(Like playing pendulum) their silver plates,
Stepping with care and listening
Hard for hid metal's cry.

It's rightly-called-chaste Belphoebe some would miss,
Some, calendar colts at Kentucky gates;
But the remotest would guess that
Some scheme's gone awry.

Danger is sunk in the pastures, the woods are sly,
Ingenuity's covered with flowers!
We thought woods were wise but never
Implicated, never involved.

Cows in mid-munch go splattered over the sky;
Roses like brush-whores smile from bowers;
Shepherds must learn a new language; this
Isn't going to be quickly solved.

Sunshiny field grass, the woods floor, are so mixed up
With earliest trusts, you have to pick back
Far past all you have learned, to go
Disinherit the dumb child,

Tell him to trust things alike and never to stop
Emptying things, but not let them lack
Love in some manner restored; to be
Sure the whole world's wild.

POTATO

for *André du Bouchet*

An underground grower, blind and a common brown;
Got a misshapen look, it's nudged where it could;
Simple as soil yet crowded as earth with all.

Cut open raw, it looses a cool clean stench,
Mineral acid seeping from pores of prest meal;
It is like breaching a strangely refreshing tomb:

Therein the taste of first stones, the hands of dead slaves,
Waters men drank in the earliest frightful woods,
Flint chips, and peat, and the cinders of buried camps.

Scrubbed under faucet water the planet skin
Polishes yellow, but tears to the plain insides;
Parching, the white's blue-hearted like hungry hands.

All of the cold dark kitchens, and war-frozen gray
Evening at window; I remember so many
Peeling potatoes quietly into chipt pails.

"It was potatoes saved us, they kept us alive."
Then they had something to say akin to praise
For the mean earth-apples, too common to cherish or steal.

Times being hard, the Sikh and the Senegalese,
Hobo and Okie, the body of Jesus the Jew,
Vestigial virtues, are eaten; we shall survive.

What has not lost its savor shall hold us up,
And we are praising what saves us, what fills the need.
(Soon there'll be packets again, with Algerian fruits.)

Oh, it will not bear polish, the ancient potato,
Needn't be nourished by Caesars, will blow anywhere,
Hidden by nature, counted-on, stubborn and blind.

You may have noticed the bush that it pushes to air,
Comical-delicate, sometimes with second-rate flowers
Awkward and milky and beautiful only to hunger.

FIRST SNOW IN ALSACE

The snow came down last night like moths
Burned on the moon; it fell till dawn,
Covered the town with simple cloths.

Absolute snow lies rumpled on
What shellbursts scattered and deranged,
Entangled railings, crevassed lawn.

As if it did not know they'd changed,
Snow smoothly clasps the roofs of homes
Fear-gutted, trustless and estranged.

The ration stacks are milky domes;
Across the ammunition pile
The snow has climbed in sparkling combs.

You think: beyond the town a mile
Or two, this snowfall fills the eyes
Of soldiers dead a little while.

Persons and persons in disguise,
Walking the new air white and fine,
Trade glances quick with shared surprise.

At children's windows, heaped, benign,
As always, winter shines the most,
And frost makes marvelous designs.

The night guard coming from his post,
Ten first-snows back in thought, walks slow
And warms him with a boyish boast:

He was the first to see the snow.

ON THE EYES
OF AN SS OFFICER

I think of Amundsen, enormously bit
By arch-dark flurries on the ice plateaus,
An amorist of violent virgin snows
At the cold end of the world's spit.

Or a Bombay saint asquat in the market place,
Eyes gone from staring the sun over the sky,
Who still dead-reckons that acetylene eye,
An eclipsed mind in a blind face.

But this one's iced or ashen eyes devise,
Foul purities, in flesh their wilderness,
Their fire; I ask my makeshift God of this
My opulent bric-a-brac earth to damn his eyes.

PLACE PIGALLE

Now homing tradesmen scatter through the streets
Toward suppers, thinking on improved conditions,
While evening, with a million simple fissions,
Takes up its warehouse watches, storefront beats,
By nursery windows its assigned positions.

Now at the corners of the Place Pigalle
Bright bars explode against the dark's embraces;
The soldiers come, the boys with ancient faces,
Seeking their ancient friends, who stroll and loll
Amid the glares and glass: electric graces.

The puppies are asleep, and snore the hounds;
But here wry hares, the soldier and the whore,
Mark off their refuge with a gaudy door,
Brazen at bay, and boldly out of bounds:
The puppies dream, the hounds superbly snore.

Ionized innocence: this pair reclines,
She on the table, he in a tilting chair,
With Arden ease; her eyes as pale as air
Travel his priestgoat face; his hand's thick tines
Touch the gold whorls of her Corinthian hair.

"Girl, if I love thee not, then let me die;
Do I not scorn to change my state with kings?
Your muchtouched flesh, incalculable, which wrings
Me so, now shall I gently seize in my
Desperate soldier's hands which kill all things."

VIOLET AND JASPER

Outside, the heirs of purity pick by,
Pecked by petite damnations, sweatless still
Along the burning marle of Cambridge; here
The light that spanks the windows takes a spill
Over the lint-bright curtain to the floor
Or frays through glasses, curly as a vine.

Broad Violet, her lettuce head all full
Of bawdry and novenas, yanks the tap,
Carries a beer to Jasper where he dreams
Of lucky numbers, falls upon his lap:
Her wandy fingers paddling on his dome
Trouble the face of El Dorado's pool.

Rumors of plenty flutter these around,
Riot, mercy and treasure haven here,
In silly brains monastically kept,
In Cambridge, where I homing saw appear
In a pharmacy window-globe ruddily rapt
Suddenly streaming with blood this turnip town.

THE PEACE OF CITIES

Terrible streets, the manichee hell of twilight
Glides like a giant bass between your windows,

Dark deploying in minnows into your alleys
Stirs and hushes the reefs of scudding trash.

Withinwalls voices, past the ports and locks,
Murmur below the shifting of crockery

I know not what; the barriered day expires
In scattered sounds of dread inconsequence.

Ah, this is no andante, there will come
No primavera, there was a louder and deeper

Peace in those other cities, when silver fear
Drove the people to fields, and there they heard

The Luftwaffe waft what let the sunshine in
And blew the bolt from everybody's door.

THE GIAOUR AND THE PACHA
(Eugène Delacroix, 1856)

The Pacha sank at last upon his knee
And saw his ancient enemy reared high
In mica dust upon a horse of bronze,
The sun carousing in his either eye,

Which of a sudden clouds, and lifts away
The light of day, of triumph; and the scene
Takes tenderly the one already dead
With secret hands of strong and bitter green.

As secretly, the cloak becomes aware
Of floating, mane and tail turn tracery;
Imbedded in the air, the Giaour stares
And feels the pistol fall beside his knee.

"Is this my anger, and is this the end
Of gaudy sword and jeweled harness, joy
In strength and heat and swiftness, that I must
Now bend, and with a slaughtering shot destroy

The counterpoise of all my force and pride?
These falling hills and piteous mists; O sky,
Come loose the light of fury on this height,
That I may end the chase, and ask not why."

UP, JACK

Prince Harry turns from Percy's pouring sides,
Full of the kind of death that honor makes
By pouring all the man into an act;
So simplified by battle, he mistakes

A hibernating Jack for dead Sir John.
"Poor pumpkin, I am cold since you are done,
For if you proved but yellow pulp within,
You were this nature's kindest earthly sun."

Exit the Prince; now Jack will rise again,
No larger now, nor spun of stuff more fine,
And only to his feet, and yet a god
To our short summer days and the world's wine.

Up, Jack! For Percy sinks in darker red,
And those who walk away are dying men.
Great Falstaff (*rising*) clears his thirsty throat,
And I'm content, and Hal is hale again.

IN A BIRD SANCTUARY

Because they could not give it too much ground
they closely planted it with fir and shrub.
A plan of pathways, voted by the Club,
contrived to lead the respiter around
a mildly wandring wood, still at no cost
to get him lost.

Now over dear Miss Drury's favored trees
they flutter (birds) and either stop or not,
as if they were unconscious that the spot
is planned for them, and meant to buy release
for one restrained department of the soul,
to "make men whole."

It's hard to tell the purpose of a bird;
for relevance it does not seem to try.
No line can trace no flute exemplify
its traveling; it darts without the word.
Who wills devoutly to absorb, contain,
birds give him pain.

Commissoners of Public Parks have won
a partial wisdom, know that birds exist.
And seeing people equally insist
on birds and statues, they go hire a man
to swab sans rancor dung from granite stare
and marble hair.

BIRDS HAVE BEEN SEEN IN TOWERS AND ON ISLES;
ALSO ON PRIVY TOPS, IN FANEUIL HALL;
BIRDS HAVE SOME OF THEM NOT BEEN SEEN AT ALL;
BIRDS, IF THEY CARE TO, WALK ALONG IN FILE.
BIRDS DO NOT FEEL ESPECIALLY GOOD IN FLIGHT:
LET'S TREAT THEM RIGHT!

The liberty of any things becomes
the liberty of all. It also brings
their abolition into anythings.
In order's name let's not turn down our thumbs
on routine visions; we must figure out
what all's about.

JUNE LIGHT

Your voice, with clear location of June days,
Called me—outside the window. You were there,
Light yet composed, as in the just soft stare
Of uncontested summer all things raise
Plainly their seeming into seamless air.

Then your love looked as simple and entire
As that picked pear you tossed me, and your face
As legible as pearskin's fleck and trace,
Which promise always wine, by mottled fire
More fatal fleshed than ever human grace.

And your gay gift—Oh when I saw it fall
Into my hands, through all that naïve light,
It seemed as blessed with truth and new delight
As must have been the first great gift of all.

A SONG

As at the bottom of a seething well
A phosphorus girl is singing,
Up whispering galleries trellised notes
Climb and cling.

It is a summer-song an old man wrote
Out of the winter's wringing,
He hunched in a cold room, back to frost's
Sledge and sting.

Desperate, gentle, every phrase declines
As fruit to groundward weighs,
As all things seek their shadows, yearn,
Yearn and fall.

She may be singing Iowa afternoons,
Lightshifting corn ballets,
Scattering stutter of windmills, each throat's
Very clear call;

Nevertheless, the balconies are in tune
And all but a single child
Are hushed in sweet relinquishing, in
Praise of time.

But the white child is puzzled, cannot hear,
To loss not reconciled
Has heartroom still for sorrows, needs no
Song or rhyme.

THE WALGH-VOGEL

More pleasurable to look than feed upon,
Hence unconserved in dodo-runs, the round,
Unfeathered, melancholy, more than fifty pound
Dodo is gone,

Who when incarnate wore two token wings
And dined on rocks, to mock at mockeries.
Empowered now by absence, blessed with tireless ease,
It soars and sings

Elated in our skies, wherever seen.
Absolute retractility allows
Its wings be wavy wide as heaven; silence endows
Its hoots serene

With airy spleenlessness all may unhear.
Alive the dodo strove for lack of point,
Extinct won superfluity, and can disjoint
To joy our fear.

Dive, dodo, on the earth you left forlorn,
Sit vastly on the branches of our trees,
And chant us grandly all improbabilities.

THE MELONGENE

Our uncrowned kings have no such regal rind
As this; their purple stain
Is in the mind.
God was more kind to this wronged kingly fruit
And pedigreed it plain.
It makes no suit

For rule in gardens, yields to the Brussels sprout,
Knows that the scornful sun
Will seek it out
In exile, and so blazon in its sheen
That it may cow and stun
Turnip and bean.

Natural pomp! Excessive Nightshades' Prince!
Polished potato, you wear
An Egyptian rinse
Of Belladonna's hues, a crown that's green,
And do not have the care
Of storing spleen,

Because your purple presence is reproof!
Before God gave him rue
And raised the roof,
Unoriginal Adam, bloat with cant
Celestial, christened you
The *Egg*-plant.

OBJECTS

Meridians are a net
Which catches nothing; that sea-scampering bird
The gull, though shores lapse every side from sight, can yet
Sense him to land, but Hanno had not heard

Hesperidean song,
Had he not gone by watchful periploi:
Chalk rocks, and isles like beasts, and mountain stains along
The water-hem, calmed him at last near-by

The clear high hidden chant
Blown from the spellbound coast, where under drifts
Of sunlight, under plated leaves, they guard the plant
By praising it. Among the wedding gifts

Of Herë, were a set
Of golden McIntoshes, from the Greek
Imagination. Guard and gild what's common, and forget
Uses and prices and names; have objects speak.

There's classic and there's quaint,
And then there is that devout intransitive eye
Of Pieter de Hooch: see feinting from his plot of paint
The trench of light on boards, the much-mended dry

Courtyard wall of brick,
And sun submerged in beer, and streaming in glasses,
The weave of a sleeve, the careful and undulant tile. A quick
Change of the eye and all this calmly passes

Into a day, into magic.
For is there any end to true textures, to true
Integuments; do they ever desist from tacit, tragic
Fading away? Oh maculate, cracked, askew,

Gay-pocked and potsherd world
I voyage, where in every tangible tree
I see afloat among the leaves, all calm and curled,
The Cheshire smile which sets me fearfully free.

A DUTCH COURTYARD

What wholly blameless fun
To stand and look at pictures. Ah, they are
Immune to us. This courtyard may appear
To be consumed with sun,

Most mortally to burn,
Yet it is quite beyond the reach of eyes
Or thoughts, this place and moment oxidize;
This girl will never turn,

Cry what you dare, but smiles
Tirelessly toward the seated cavalier,
Who will not proffer you his pot of beer;
And your most lavish wiles

Can never turn this chair
To proper uses, nor your guile evict
These tenants. What surprising strict
Propriety! In despair,

Consumed with greedy ire,
Old Andrew Mellon glowered at this Dutch
Courtyard, until it bothered him so much
He bought the thing entire.

MY FATHER PAINTS THE SUMMER

A smoky rain riddles the ocean plains,
Rings on the beaches' stones, stomps in the swales,
Batters the panes
Of the shore hotel, and the hoped-for summer chills and fails.
The summer people sigh,
"Is this July?"

They talk by the lobby fire but no one hears
For the thrum of the rain. In the dim and sounding halls,
Din at the ears,
Dark at the eyes well in the head, and the ping-pong balls
Scatter their hollow knocks
Like crazy clocks.

But up in his room by artificial light
My father paints the summer, and his brush
Tricks into sight
The prosperous sleep, the girdling stir and clear steep hush
Of a summer never seen,
A granted green.

Summer, luxuriant Sahara, the orchard spray
Gales in the Eden trees, the knight again
Can cast away
His burning mail, Rome is at Anzio: but the rain
For the ping-pong's optative bop
Will never stop.

Caught Summer is always an imagined time.
Time gave it, yes, but time out of any mind.
There must be prime
In the heart to beget that season, to reach past rain and find
Riding the palest days
Its perfect blaze.

FOLK TUNE

When Bunyan swung his whopping axe
The forests strummed as one loud lute,
The timber crashed beside his foot
And sprung up stretching in his tracks.

He had an ox, but his was blue.
The flower in his buttonhole
Was brighter than a parasol.
He's gone. Tom Swift has vanished too,

Who worked at none but wit's expense,
Putting dirigibles together
Out in the yard, in the quiet weather,
Whistling behind Tom Sawyer's fence.

Now when the darkness in my street
Nibbles the last and crusty crumbs
Of sound, and all the city numbs
And goes to sleep upon its feet,

I listen hard to hear its dreams:
John Henry is our nightmare friend,
Whose shoulders roll without an end,
Whose veins pump, pump and burst their seams,

Whose sledge is smashing at the rock
And makes the sickly city toss
And half awake in sighs of loss
Until the screaming of the clock.

John Henry's hammer and his will
Are here and ringing out our wrong,
I hear him driving all night long
To beat the leisured snarling drill.

SUN AND AIR

The air staggers under the sun, and heat-morasses
Flutter the birds down; wind barely climbs the hills,
Saws thin and splinters among the roots of the grasses;

All stir sickens, and falls into barn shadows, spills
Into hot hay and heat-hammered road dust, makes no sound,
Waiting the sun's siege out to collect its wills.

As a hound stretched sleeping will all on a sudden bound,
Air will arise all sinews, crack-crying, tear tether,
Plow sheets of powder high, heave sky from milling ground.

So sun and air, when these two goods war together,
Who else can tune day's face to a softest laugh,
Being sweet beat the world with a most wild weather,

Trample with light or blow all heaven blind with chaff.

TWO SONGS IN A
STANZA OF BEDDOES'

1

That lavished sunlight, where
And lilac-mottled air,
And where the fair-skinned winds
    That touched the plum
To fall? All gone; my mind's
Lost all the summer, binds
    No beauty home.

How have such seas of sun
Cast me so dry here? Run,
Mindseye, and find a field
    Embered with clover . . .
Why is my heart congealed,
All the sweet season sealed
    Off from her lover?

Stretch, tamarack, and strain;
Lash, poplar; and complain,
Guttering grasses; seek
    For summer, swallow:
And mind, fill full of creak
And hustling scraps, be bleak
    And howling-hollow.

Come tender winter, weep
This raving earth to sleep;
Your deadly tears disguise
    In lightest white.
Frost these forgetful eyes
From day's sheet-metal skies
    And viselike night.

2

Through tossing views, the gull,
All-balancing, can scull
The sky, and strew its calls
    On the breeze;
Its shivered shadow crawls
The leisured azure brawls
    Of the seas.

When then from day's blue brink
Its rapt reflections sink,
A bird made dark, unclear,
    To sea-deep flies,
And monstrous flutters there,
And slow and loud with fear
    Cries and cries.

THE WATERS

From powdery Palmyre, the tireless wind,
Braided by waves but cradling to this shore,
Where folding water leaves Atlantis' gold,
Dust of Aurelian's sack, scrawls in the sand,
Streams in the salty grass the stainless cries
Of fighters at the gate, and strews the trees
With, milled by many days, Zenobia's priceless robe.

And the sunned wind, as the wave thins and slips
Into rock-pools, lies in the shallows of the spine.
And the mind, as the sand rises and rolls in the pull
Of the wave, yields to the cry of the buried child.

The sea so sings us back to histories
On every perilous beach. At Juan-les-Pins
Or Coney Isle, the bathers lie between
Yellow and blue, in the handling of such soft air
That real caresses leaf the thinnest hair,
Maternal murmurs sweep the dozing head;
And gazing out from underneath our arms,
We see the spring of feet from brightened sand;
We feel the world lie warm beneath the hand;
And hear the cry of voices over water,
Or horns of vessels very far from land.

And only the dull are safe, only the dead
Are safe from the limitless swell and the bitter seethe,
The sea's lumbering sigh that says it carries
So many stars and suns, and yet will wreathe
A rock with webs of foam and maidenhair.
Von Aschenbach, when he perceived the fair
Aureate child before the endless sea,
Shingled his painted face in agony.

For the damnedest lovers of water dread the waves:
The inland painters in whose canvases
We read some vaporized and fierce devotion
To "the smiling of women, and the motion
Of great waters"; the pauper poet who dreamed
Of sunken rivers, yet who scorned to seek
Their sources in the caves of the world; and he
Who mad and weak, became a sailingcraft
On heilignüchterne lakes of memory.

SUPERIORITIES

Malachy stamped the diving decks
And shouted to the frigging wind
"Frig on!," and hove an empty quart
Into the stomach of a wave.

Phipps at the bucking rail was still
And keenly modest as a star,
Attentive to each blast and surge,
And so becalmed the storm in him.

How far superior to those
Huddled below with wives and buddies,
Comforting, caring, sharing pills,
Prayers and other proper studies.

A SIMPLIFICATION

Those great rough ranters, Branns
And catarrhal Colonels, who hurled
Terrible taunts at the vault, ripped down Jesus' banns
And widowed the world

With Inquisitorial thunder, dammed-
Up Biblical damnations, were
The last with tongues to topple heaven; they hammered
Jahweh away and here

We are. The decorous god
Simply withdrew. If you hear
A good round rhetoric anywhere give me the nod.
I'd like to hear

Bryan lying and quoting sic
Transit nux vomica. These foetal-
Voiced people lack eloquence to blow a sick
Maggot off a dead beetle.

A DUBIOUS NIGHT

A bell diphthonging in an atmosphere
Of shying night air summons some to prayer
Down in the town, two deep lone miles from here,

Yet wallows faint or sudden everywhere,
In every ear, as if the twist wind wrung
Some ten years' tangled echoes from the air.

What kyries it says are mauled among
The queer elisions of the mist and murk,
Of lights and shapes; the senses were unstrung,

Except that one star's synecdochic smirk
Burns steadily to me, that nothing's odd
And firm as ever is the masterwork.

I weary of the confidence of God.

L'ETOILE
(Degas, 1876)

A rushing music, seizing on her dance,
Now lifts it from her, blind into the light;
And blind the dancer, tiptoe on the boards
Reaches a moment toward her dance's flight.

Even as she aspires in loudening shine
The music pales and sweetens, sinks away;
And past her arabesque in shadow show
The fixt feet of the maître de ballet.

So she will turn and walk through metal halls
To where some ancient woman will unmesh
Her small strict shape, and yawns will turn her face
Into a little wilderness of flesh.

SUNLIGHT IS IMAGINATION

Each shift you make in the sunlight somewhere
Cleaves you away into dark. Now
You are clarion hair, bright brow,
Lightcaped shoulder and armside here, and there
Gone into meadow shadow. Where
Are my eyes to run?
Shall I say you are fair
In the sun,
Or mermaid you in the grass waving away?

Shall I say
The whole green day builds hither to lift
This flare of your hair?, I wielding such sight
As did Juan Ponce, climbing to light
On a morning of the Feast of the Resurrection. Aloft
On the ocean shelf he saw the soft
Signals of trees
And gulls, and the sift
Of the sea's
Long landward airs offering trails to him.

And dim
Each flower of Florida, but all
Was shining; parrots prophesied;
Vines ciphered; to each waterside
Paths pitched in hopes to the fair and noble well
Of sweetest savor and reflaire
Whose ghostly taste
And cleanse repair
All waste,
And where was ageless power from the first.

Yet thirst
  Makes deserts, barrens to a sign
  Deckled and delicate arbors, bleeds
  The rose, parches the prodigal seeds
  That spring toward time in air, and breaks the spine
  Of the rock. No; I shall resign
  That power, and crave
  Kindly to pine
  And to save
  The sprout and the ponderation of the land.

My hand
  Can touch but mysteries, and each
  Of a special shadow. I shall spare
  The larch its shattering ghost, the pear
  Its dark awaiter too, for shades beseech
  Originals: they running reach
  On windy days
  To touch, to teach
  What stays
  Is changed, and shadows die into dying things.

Now swings
  The sky to noon, and mysteries run
  To cover; let our love not blight
  The various world, but trust the flight
  Of love that falls again where it begun.
  All creatures are, and are undone.
  Then lose them, lose
  With love each one,
  And choose
  To welcome love in the lively wasting sun.

A slopeshouldered shape from scurrying burdens
Backward and forth, or perhaps a lyre
Or a clef wrung wry in tuning untunable tones,
Or a knot for tugging an out-of-hand

Vine to the trellis in clerical gardens:
Sweetness & light, ice & fire,
Nature & art have dissocketed all your bones,
Porter, poor pander ampersand,

O

The idle dayseye, the laborious wheel,
The osprey's tours, the pointblank matin sun
Sanctified first the circle; thence for fun
Doctors deduced a shape, which some called real
(So all games spoil), a shape of spare appeal,
Cryptic and clean, and endlessly spinning unspun.
Now I go backward, filling by one and one
Circles with hickory spokes and rich soft shields
Of petalled dayseyes, with herehastening steel
Volleys of daylight, writhing white looks of sun;
And I toss circles skyward to be undone
By actual wings, for wanting this repeal
I should go whirling a thin Euclidean reel,
No hawk or hickory to true my run.

THE REGATTA

A rowdy wind pushed out the sky,
Now swoops the lake and booms in sails;
Sunlight can plummet, when it fails,
Brighten on boats which pitch and fly.

Out on the dock-end, Mrs. Vane,
Seated with friends, lifts lenses to
Delighted eyes, and sweeps the view
Of "galleons" on the "raging main."

A heeling boat invades the glass
To turn a buoy; figures duck
The crossing sail—"There's Midge and Buck!
I know his scarf!"—the sailors pass.

The hotel guests make joking bets,
And Mrs. Vane has turned, inquired
If Mr. Vane is feeling "tired."
He means to answer, but forgets.

She offers him binoculars:
A swift, light thing is slipping on
The bitter waters, always gone
Before the wave can make it hers;

So simply it evades, evades,
So weightless and immune may go,
The free thing does not need to know
How deep the waters are with shades.

It's but a trick; and still one feels
Franchised a little—God knows I
Would be the last alive to cry
To Whatzisname, "I love thy wheels!"

Freedom's a pattern. I am cold.
I don't know what I'm doing here.
And Mrs. Vane says, "Home now, dear."
He rises, does as he is told;
Hugging her arm, he climbs the pier.
Behind him breaks the triumph cheer.

BELL SPEECH

The selfsame toothless voice for death or bridal:
It has been long since men would give the time
To tell each someone's-change with a special chime,
And a toll for every year the dead walked through.
And mostly now, above this urgent idle
Town, the bells mark time, as they can do.

This bavardage of early and of late
Is what is wanted, and yet the bells beseech
By some excess that's in their stricken speech
Less meanly to be heard. Were this not so,
Why should Great Paul shake every window plate
To warn me that my pocket watch is slow?

Whether or not attended, bells will chant
With a clear dumb sound, and wide of any word
Expound our hours, clear as the waves are heard
Crashing at Mount Desert, from far at sea,
And dumbly joining, as the night's descent
Makes deltas into dark of every tree.

Great Paul, great pail of sound, still dip and draw
Dark speech from the deep and quiet steeple well,
Bring dark for doctrine, do but dim and quell
All voice in yours, while earth will give you breath.
Still gather to a language without flaw
Our loves, and all the hours of our death.

POPLAR, SYCAMORE

Poplar, absolute danseuse,
Wind-wed and faithless to wind, troweling air
Tinily everywhere faster than air can fill,
Here whitely rising, there
Winding, there
Feinting to earth with a greener spill,
Never be still, whose pure mobility
Can hold up crowding heaven with a tree.

Sycamore, trawled by the tilt sun,
Still scrawl your trunk with tattered lights, and keep
The spotted toad upon your patchy bark,
Baffle the sight to sleep,
Be such a deep
Rapids of lacing light and dark,
My eye will never know the dry disease
Of thinking things no more than what he sees.

WINTER SPRING

A script of trees before the hill
Spells cold, with laden serifs; all the walls
Are battlemented still;
But winter spring is winnowing the air
Of chill, and crawls
Wet-sparkling on the gutters;
Everywhere
Walls wince, and there's the steal of waters.

Now all this proud royaume
Is Veniced. Through the drift's mined dome
One sees the rowdy rusted grass,
And we're amazed as windows stricken bright.
This too-soon spring will pass
Perhaps tonight,
And doubtless it is dangerous to love
This somersault of seasons;
But I am weary of
The winter way of loving things for reasons.

ATTENTION MAKES INFINITY

The kingdom of air, of lightly looming air
That crowns us all king spinners, let it swing
Wide of the earth and any foundering
In the sea's reflection, the forest's manifold snare.

Air is refreshment's treasury; earth seems
Our history's faulted sink, and spring of love;
And we between these dreamt-of empires move
To coop infinity away from dreams.

See, every yard, alive with laundry white,
Billowing wives and leaves, gives way to air;
A blown pedestrian upon the square
Tosses a clanging trolley out of sight.

Then air relents to skyward with a sigh,
Earth's adamant variety is remade;
The hanging dust above the streets is staid
And solid as the walls of Central High.

Contagions of the solid make this day
An infiniteness any eye may prove.
Let asphalt bear us up to walk in love,
Electric towers shore the clouds away.

GRACE

So active they seem passive, little sheep
Please, and Nijinsky's out-the-window leap
And marvelous midair pause please too
A taste for blithe brute reflex; flesh made word
Is grace's revenue.

One is tickled, again, by the dining-car waiter's absurd
Acrobacy—tipfingered tray like a wind-besting bird
Plumblines his swinging shoes, the sole things sure
In the shaken train; but this is all done for food,
Is habitude, if not pure

Hebetude. It is a graph of a theme that flings
The dancer kneeling on nothing into the wings,
And Nijinsky hadn't the words to make the laws
For learning to loiter in air; he "merely" said,
"I merely leap and pause."

Lambs are constrained to bound. Consider instead
The intricate neural grace in Hamlet's head;
A grace not barbarous implies a choice
Of courses, not in a lingo of leaps-in-air
But in such a waiting voice

As one would expect to hear in the talk of Flaubert.
Piety makes for awkwardness, and where
Balance is not urgent, what one utters
May be puzzled and perfect, and we respect
Some scholars' stutters.

Even fraction-of-a-second action is not wrecked
By a graceful still reserve. To be unchecked
Is needful then: choose, challenge, jump, poise, run. . . .
Nevertheless, the praiseful, graceful soldier
Shouldn't be fired by his gun.

LIGHTNESS

A birdsnest built on the palm of the high-
Most bough of an elm, this morning as I came by
A brute gust lifted-and-left in the midst of the air;
    Whereat the leaves went quiet, and there
    Was a moment of silence in honor of
The sweetness of danger. The chalice now bobbing above,
Of interlaid daintiest timber, began the chute
    Down forty fell feet toward stone and root
    With a drift and a sampan spin, and gripped
Loosely its fineshelled life; now viciously tipped
By a ripple of air, with an acrobat's quick not-quite-
    Lost, dipped lower to whirl upright;
    Then, with a straight-down settling, it
Descended into sunshine, and, with a hushed touch, lit
On a mesa of strenuous grass. Oh risk-hallowed eggs, oh
    Triumph of lightness! Legerity begs no
    Quarter: my Aunt Virginia, when
She'd relapsed and recovered, would sit in the garden again
Waiting, all lapped in an indigo-flowered shawl,
    In white for her "regular customers' " call;
    Whose pity she parried with very-blue-eyed
Attention, and giggled and patted their hands when they tried
To do-something-for-her; she sat in the heart of her days
    And watched with a look of peculiar praise;
    Her slight voice could catch a pleasure complete
As a gull takes a fish at the flash of his side. Her great
Heavy husband adored her, would treat with a sudden blind sally
    Of softness his "visitor from the valley";
    He called her "Birdie," which was good, for him.
And he and the others, the strong, the involved, in-the-swim,
Seeing her there in the garden, in her gay shroud
    As vague and as self-possessed as a cloud,
    Requiring nothing of them any more,
And one hand lightly laid on a fatal door,
Thought of the health of the sick, and, what mocked their sighing,
    Of the strange intactness of the gladly dying.

FOR ELLEN

On eyes embarked for sleep the only light
Goes off, and there is nothing that you know
So well, it may not monster in this sea.
The vine leaves pat the screen. Viciously free,
The wind vaults over the roof with Mister Crow
To drop his crooked laughter in your night.

And morning's cannonades of brightness come
To a little utter blueness in your eyes.
You stagger goldenly, bestowing blue;
Blue heal-all breaks the pavingstone where you
Expect it, and you laugh in pure surprise
At the comic cripple hurdling to his slum.

But sometime you will look at the lazy sun
Hammocked in clouds, dead-slumbering in the sky.
That casual fire will blister blue, and night
Will strand its fears; then with a starker sight
And newer darker love, you will supply
The world of joy which never was begun.

CASERTA GARDEN

Their garden has a silent tall stone-wall
So overburst with drowsing trees and vines,
None but a stranger would remark at all
The barrier within the fractured lines.

I doubt they know it's there, or what it's for—
To keep the sun-impasted road apart,
The beggar, soldier, renegade and whore,
The dust, the sweating ox, the screeching cart.

They'd say, "But this is how a garden's made":
To fall through days in silence dark and cool,
And hear the fountain falling in the shade
Tell changeless time upon the garden pool.

See from the tiptoe boy—the dolphin throats—
The fine spray bending; jets collapse in rings
Into the round pool, and each circle floats
Wide to the verge, and fails in shimmerings.

A childhood by this fountain wondering
Would leave impress of circle-mysteries:
One would have faith that the unjustest thing
Had geometric grace past what one sees.

How beauties will grow richer walled about!
This tortile trunk, old paradigm of pain,
These cherished flowers—they dream and look not out,
And seem to have no need of earth or rain.

In heavy peace, walled out necessity,
How devious the lavish grapevine crawls,
And trails its shade, irrelevant and free,
In delicate cedillas on the walls.

And still without, the dusty shouting way,
Hills lazar-skinned, with hungry-rooted trees,
And towns of men, below a staring day,
Go scattered to the turning mountain frieze.

The garden of the world, which no one sees,
Never had walls, is fugitive with lives;
Its shapes escape our simpler symmetries;
There is no resting where it rots and thrives.

PRAISE IN SUMMER

Obscurely yet most surely called to praise,
As sometimes summer calls us all, I said
The hills are heavens full of branching ways
Where star-nosed moles fly overhead the dead;
I said the trees are mines in air, I said
See how the sparrow burrows in the sky!
And then I wondered why this mad *instead*
Perverts our praise to uncreation, why
Such savor's in this wrenching things awry.
Does sense so stale that it must needs derange
The world to know it? To a praiseful eye
Should it not be enough of fresh and strange
That trees grow green, and moles can course in clay,
And sparrows sweep the ceiling of our day?

THE BEAUTIFUL CHANGES

One wading a Fall meadow finds on all sides
The Queen Anne's Lace lying like lilies
On water; it glides
So from the walker, it turns
Dry grass to a lake, as the slightest shade of you
Valleys my mind in fabulous blue Lucernes.

The beautiful changes as a forest is changed
By a chameleon's tuning his skin to it;
As a mantis, arranged
On a green leaf, grows
Into it, makes the leaf leafier, and proves
Any greenness is deeper than anyone knows.

Your hands hold roses always in a way that says
They are not only yours; the beautiful changes
In such kind ways,
Wishing ever to sunder
Things and things' selves for a second finding, to lose
For a moment all that it touches back to wonder.

Notes

MINED COUNTRY: *Silver Plates:* mine detectors.

UP, JACK: *King Henry IV, Part I*, Act V, Scene 4.

THE WALGH-VOGEL: Title and first stanza derived from Sir Thomas Herbert's *Travels*, quoted in Phipson's *Animal-Lore of Shakspeare's Time.*

OBJECTS: *A Dutch Courtyard*, by Pieter de Hooch, is in the National Gallery at Washington.

THE WATERS: The last section refers to Leonardo via Walter Pater, Villiers de l'Isle Adam, and Holderlin. These artists, particularly the two last, seem to me to have suffered similar emotional tragedies.

A SIMPLIFICATION: Brann the iconoclast was shot dead on the streets of Waco in 1898. Not an important figure, but his name has the irascible sound I was seeking.